JESUS LOVES MOVIES

A 30 Day Devotional for Film Fans

Phil Strangolagalli

ACKNOWLEDGMENTS

To my wonderful wife, Kathryn, who has helped me along the journey of writing this book and making it happen. I love being married to you! It's the best thing ever! Thank you for loving me with such incredible love and for believing in me. Thank you for helping me edit in the midst of your busy schedule.

To the best dad in the world. You have been here for me and helped me when times were tough. I love you and I hope this book makes you proud!

To the best mom! You're so supportive and I love you! You bring such a comfort to me.

To my brother, my best friend. You're the best brother anyone could ask for!

To Casey, thank you for being willing to help edit this precious project! Excited for your poetry to come out soon! Follow her @adellecasey

To Nyack College, I grew so much there! Thank you for letting me be free in worshipping God creatively.

To all who have supported me, thank you...this includes you.

To God above all.

CONTENTS

Introduction	7
Toy story (1995)	9
Wreck-It Ralph (2012)	13
Shawshank Redemption (1994)	17
The Count Of Monte Cristo (2002)	21
The Guardians of the Galaxy (2014)	27
A Place Beyond the Pines (2012)	31
Zootopia (2016)	35
The Rookie (2002)	39
The Sandlot (1993)	43
The Babadook (2014)	47
Inside Out (2015)	53
The Revenant (2015)	57
Groundhog Day (1993)	63
Frozen (2013)	69

Ratatouille (2007)   73

Ant-Man (2015)   79

Spider-Man: Homecoming (2017)   83

Mean Girls (2004)   87

Wonder Woman (2017)   91

Hacksaw Ridge (2016)   97

Split (2017)   103

Monsters Incorporated (2001)   107

Real Steel (2011)   113

Star Wars Episode V: The Empire Strikes Back (1980)   119

Sinister (2012)   123

Doctor Strange (2016)   129

The Prestige (2006)   135

The Gift (2015)   141

Cinderella (2015)   147

The Wizard of Oz (1939)   151

INTRODUCTION

Movies are my love language with God. It wasn't always this way, I had put God in a box at one point of my journey—He was only in the Bible and nowhere else. But my prayer is that as you read this, you would hear and see God in a brand new way. That you would know that He is in all good things, that He can surprise you, by showing up in anything. So, read this as a 30 day devotional, a book, a yearly reflection, whatever you like, make it yours. May it be a space where He meets you in intimacy, and where you hear Him speak your language.

So, use this book however you wish, but I suggest if you really want to dive into seeing God in the movies, watch some of these films, put yourself in the character's shoes, and let Him speak into your heart. Then, ask God if there are some movies that He wants you to watch, or rewatch. Try it, and then invite Him into that. He is personal, and cares about what you care about (I have found Him in some of the horror movies I have wrote about in here, but I get it if you're like my wife and don't enjoy their artistic anointing).

I wrote this book from my pain; I had never planned on writing it. It consists of the lessons, the revelations, the deep things I experienced during one of the hardest times of my life. It was during this time, that God whispered to me through movies, and this is what He showed me through them.

I have prayed through how I wanted to order each of the films in this book, and I hope that you can find the easter eggs along the way.

TOY STORY (1995)

*And the scripture was fulfilled that says,
"Abraham believed God, and it was credited
to him as righteousness," and he was called
God's friend. James 2:23 NIV*

Meet Woody, a cowboy toy and Andy's (Woody's owner) prized possession. Andy and Woody were inseparable. Andy played with Woody all the time. Woody loved being Andy's favorite toy. Andy loved Woody so much, he even had Woody-themed wallpaper in his bedroom, Woody-themed bedding, and everything in between. These were the glory days, until...*Buzz Lightyear ruined it all.*

Woody was no longer Andy's favorite.

Woody's friendship with Andy had dissipated into infinity and beyond. He had lost his best friend, the one who would give him piggyback rides and would dress up to look just like Woody. Basically, when Buzz came into the picture, Woody's life was over. In Woody's eyes, his friendship with Andy had died. He was no longer Andy's favorite. He had been replaced.

Put yourself in Woody's boots. Imagine the loneliness, rejection, and abandonment he experienced. Andy had once written his name on the bottom of Woody's boot, and it was now wearing off, while Buzz's boot had a fresh imprinted signature.

There are times we feel that God has completely abandoned us, like He is off in the distance, busy with something or someone else. Or, we feel rejection and disapproval from other people.

Your feelings are valid. Life is tough. In these circumstances, and wherever you are in life, I want to remind you that you are God's prized possession. God's name is imprinted on you and it's never going to fade away. You are His.

You might feel like Woody, yearning for your Owner's attention, and unlike Andy, your Father *always* wants to give you a piggyback ride and take you on a journey. God wants you to know that He will never leave you or reject you. He always sings: "You got a friend in Me."

WRECK-IT RALPH (2012)

The stone that the builders rejected has
become the cornerstone. Psalm 118:22 ESV

Fix-It Felix Jr. is the name of the video game. Wreck-It Ralph is the "bad guy" and his job is to destroy a building and wreak havoc like Donkey Kong. The mission of the gamer is to use Fix-It Felix Jr.'s magic hammer to clean up Ralph's mess, repair the building, and save the Nicelanders from Ralph's destruction and terror! Once victory is achieved, Felix gets a shiny golden medal, while Ralph is tossed by the townspeople into mud. Ralph gets no positive recognition. His only purpose? That of a pawn—one which provides the framework for Felix's victory medal. When gametime ends, and the arcade closes, Ralph remains the villain while Felix, his medal, and the Nicelanders celebrate with a party. Ralph is left uninvited, and covers himself in his blanket made of rubble as he goes to sleep.

Unlike most stereotypical bad guys, Ralph wants deep down more than anything to be accepted and loved. Ralph even says that he feels rejected and like a criminal everyday of his life. The truth is that the Nicelanders don't understand Ralph: 'He is supposed to be the villain who reigns terror on the townspeople, he is not supposed to have a heart. He should be angry, shallow, and villainous.'

He wants to prove to the Nicelanders that he CAN be good, he CAN get a medal of his own. He longs to find a medal so that he can prove himself and in turn be loved by the characters in his game. In order to do so, Ralph sets out on an excursion.

Escaping his game, Ralph makes it to Game Central Station and manages to disguise himself in order to get into another game called Hero's Duty. Ralph proves victorious and is awarded the Medal of Heroes, but not without fault.

In the midst of his victory, Wreck-It Ralph destructively steps on a Cybug and is sent via escape pod and crash lands into another game…Sugar Rush. In Sugar Rush—a Racing world filled with sweetness, colors, and fluff—Ralph encounters Vanellope Von Schweetz and his life changes forever.

Vanellope—a little girl originally designed to be a prestigious racer, lived far away from the game's fast paced action, and never stepped foot on the track. Vanellope had been given the label—glitch.

Both having lived lives as outcasts, Ralph and Vanellope bonded and found deep acceptance from their friendship. Vanellope even gave Ralph a custom made medal with the engraved message: "You're My Hero." That was all he needed—someone who would like him for who he was. Ralph finally felt like he belonged. He just needed to be accepted. It took someone else who was rejected to understand Ralph. The acceptance that Ralph was searching for had been finally been found.

"Turns out I don't need a medal to tell me I'm a good guy. Because if that little kid likes me how bad can I be?"

Do you feel like you just don't belong? That people don't understand you? Do you feel like you have to prove yourself to gain acceptance? The truth is, *you don't have to prove yourself.*

And you are not alone!

That true Someone who has been rejected and who accepts you is Jesus. Jesus was rejected in His own game. He wants you to know that you belong in Him and that you are loved by Him. He was deserted by His closest friends, He even felt like His loving Father abandoned Him. If there's anyone who understands what it means to be shoved aside, it's Jesus.

The crazy thing is, because of His rejection, you have been accepted. You're not a glitch in the system, you are not someone who just breaks everything in your path, you are deeply loved and you are *accepted* by God.

Please, remember that.

SHAWSHANK REDEMPTION (1994)

The Son of Man came eating and drinking,
and they say, 'Look at him! A glutton and
a drunkard, a friend of tax collectors and
sinners!' Yet wisdom is justified by her
deeds. Matthew 11:19 ESV

In the beginning of the movie, we see Andy Dufresne drinking whiskey in his car, holding his gun as he parks right outside of the house where his wife is committing adultery. All of the evidence points to him being the murderer of his wife and the man she was with. But the beginning of the film shows that he threw his gun into the Royal River and slept off his drunkenness. Andy was in the wrong place at the wrong time, and because of this was deemed as guilty as a sewage pipe. There he was,

Andy Dufresne, an innocent man, being sent to two life imprisonments for the murder he didn't commit.

Sexual assault, physical beatings—Andy, an innocent man, deals with the common life of an inmate. He meets a prison mate who knows the man who murdered his wife and her lover. He believes this was the key to prove his innocence. Andy's only way to freedom is botched however, when his witness becomes executed by order of the warden. The warden, a corrupt man, has no interest in Andy's side of things. Andy—a man worthy of innocence—has no shot at freedom.

Most of us know that Andy had an elaborate plan to escape from Shawshank—a truly classic evacuation. So, by using a small rock hammer to chisel a tunnel in the prison cell-wall keeping him from liberation, "Andy crawled to *freedom* through 500 yards of [sewage] smelling foulness I can't even imagine, or maybe I just don't want to..."

Imagine that...being condemned for a murder that you didn't commit. I am sure many of you have experiences of frustration, pain, and confusion to the capacity and level that Andy must have. You may have been treated unfairly, been stripped of your worth, dignity, or innocence. You could have done nothing wrong, yet you've been misjudged and deemed guilty.

Andy experiences life's crap and still finds a way out. His story teaches us that even when we're misjudged, if we hold onto hope and persevere in the midst of injustice, there's always a chance for freedom.

If there is anyone who knows what it's like to be treated unfairly, it's Jesus. He came as God in the flesh. No one recognized Him for who He really was (you know, Holy, Perfect, Righteous, Pure?). The people He created spat on Him, tortured Him, and treated Him like an outcast...Imagine that. Jesus—the most innocent and pure human to ever exist, didn't get the treatment He deserved. He was called a glutton and a drunk. He was executed, even though He was sinless and perfect.

There are chances in life when you might not be given a fair shot. Not being given a fair deal is problematic.

It hurts and it's not the justification or validation you deserve. Andy Dufresne did nothing wrong and yet, was sent to prison. There may be times in life where you are going along fine, doing nothing wrong, and out of nowhere, you are faced with injustice.

The reality is, we live in an unfair world. But don't let this turn you into a victim. Live holding onto the hope knowing that Jesus—a man condemned for innocence—understands every minute detail of what you are going through.

So, let Him comfort you. Sit quiet, He won't judge you, He won't misunderstand you, meditate on the fact that He, too, was treated unfairly, ask Him how He relates to you in this moment, and then, ask Him to meet you there.

THE COUNT OF MONTE CRISTO (2002)

*Do not take revenge, my dear friends, but
leave room for God's wrath, for it is written:
"It is mine to avenge; I will repay," says the
Lord. Romans 12:19 NIV*

Have you ever been wronged in such a way that you
only saw red, and all you wanted to do was take
revenge on those who hurt you? Has someone ever
poured salt on your wound or punched your soul in the
gut? It can be difficult to move forward, and it might
even feel impossible.

There he is, bright, handsome, and righteous: Edmond
Dantès, the highly favored and likeable young man in all
of his land. He has a beautiful fiancée, Mercédès, and
even gets promoted to captain of a ship. All is looking

21

picture-perfect for Dantès, until Fernand Mondego gets a little too close.

Mondego was that jealous friend of Dantès, and he becomes so envious of what Dantès has, that the only way he would feel better is if Dantès just wasn't around. Thus, Mondego secretly develops a plan to accuse Edmond of committing a crime. Mondego collaborates with the Chief Magistrate, Villefort, who has the power to send Edmond to prison, and then sends him off to Chateau d'If, an exiled prison island.

Don't know about you, but doesn't that sound like the experience of being in a workplace or in an office? All of a sudden, you're the new employee, and you come in all prim and proper, ready for the job, and there are people there who see how your life is going and they want to destroy you. They'll do anything to come up with any plans to control what the boss thinks of you.

So they come up with a plan to get rid of you so that they'll feel better.

I know what it's like to be treated like this. I know what it's like to have everything set, then all of a sudden, have it all ripped from me. I know what it's like to be surrounded by my friends, by a family that loves me, then get exiled to a lonely island. I know what it's like to be attacked by people for doing nothing wrong. Trust me, you're not alone.

If you've gone through any of the above, I'm pretty sure Edmond's story relates to you.

Here Edmond is, exiled and alone. I can't blame him for getting angry at the people who did him wrong. His feelings are completely valid. Wait a minute, Phil, aren't you supposed to be forgiving all the time for what people do to you? Let's be honest here; that would be easy if I were Jesus.

The fact is, it's not easy! When people wrong you or when people hurt you deeply, it's not easy at all to move forward! It took Edmond a LONG time before figuring out that committing revenge was not his place, it was God's.

JESUS LOVES MOVIES

While in prison Edmond befriends Abbé Faria, a priest that educates him, toughens him, and shepherds him. The priest gives two major pieces of advice to Edmond: the location of a treasure and the reminder that vengeance is God's and not Edmond's. Through Faria's death, Dantes is able to place himself in the sackcloth where Faria's body was laid and escapes from prison. But not really…his bitterness now held him captive.

Edmond was not a perfect human. He takes revenge on every single one of his wrongdoers. Even though one of his trusted friends, Jacopo, tells him to end taking revenge and Abbé Faria told him that vengeance was God's, Edmond realizes that he can't stop taking revenge on them. Edmond is controlled by his pain. After Edmond commits all of his revenge, we reach the end of the movie, and Edmond realizes that it was all for nothing. Revenge didn't satisfy him; it didn't fix a thing. He recalls the words of his prison friend, and surrenders: "You were right Priest." Edmond gives his bitterness to God in that moment and is finally a free man.

There will be times when people wrong you. You might have Edmond's desire to take vengeance and "give them what they deserve." Let me just say, acknowledge that you're angry with them. I think so many times we shrug our anger off and say "I have to be nice to them," cultivating all types of passivity and bitterness. In reality, that's not the best thing to do. It's important to process how you've been hurt, and to be real with yourself and with God on how badly you're in pain.

There are times when people might hurt you really badly, and the amount of stuff that comes up in your head might be unthinkable. If it takes forgiving those who have hurt you every day, every time you have a such a thought, then that's what it takes. Praying blessings over them is truly a jailbreaker, and it will set you free in the process. The amazing hope is that God instructs us that vengeance is His and He will repay the wrongdoing. He will take care of it in His own way, so confess how you feel to God.

Do you feel trapped by bitterness or resentment? If so, forgive and bless those who have hurt you. If you hold a grudge towards someone and don't forgive them, you are basically putting yourself in handcuffs. You have the key—the key is forgiveness.

"But what if the pain was too much?" You might ask. It might be, but there is no one better to validate that than Jesus. Know this about forgiveness: forgiveness does not make what happened okay. It doesn't excuse what happened to you—hear me here—forgiveness doesn't make it okay at all, but what forgiveness does is set YOU free. Free from the pain, the hurt, it helps you to really, finally, move forward. God can help you break the shackles; without Him, without choosing His grace, forgiveness is impossible.

THE GUARDIANS OF THE GALAXY (2014)

*...Jesus said to them, "Truly I tell you,
the tax collectors and the prostitutes are
entering the kingdom of God ahead of
you..." Matthew 21:31 NIV*

The kingdom of God is for the criminals.

Who were the followers of Jesus? They were a bunch of broken people. They were shame-filled people, they were scammers, they were prostitutes, they were the scraps of society.

Who are the Guardians of the Galaxy? Well, there is a scene when Korath of the Kree has a mission to retrieve an orb, but a space-cowboy makes it to the orb before him. The ex-ravager reveals his identity as Star-

Lord! Korath responds with one of the best one-liners in the film: "Who?"

Before the film's release, no one really knew anything about who the Guardians of the Galaxy were. Even characters in the film thought they were a bunch of hooligans.

Meet Star-Lord, Groot, Rocket Raccoon, Drax, and Gamora. Rocket and Groot are partner thieves, Star-Lord is a space outlaw, Drax is a man who likes vengeance, and Gamora—a former assassin—is the adopted daughter of Thanos, the 'Dark Lord' who seeks to destroy all and have ultimate power. Every one of these 'guardians' come from different criminal backgrounds, yet we see them become unlikely heroes. These five culprits find themselves in unexpected circumstances, which leads them to save the galaxy from Ronan the Accuser, a power-hungry villain seeking its destruction.

In the Bible, we have Saul, who later becomes Paul—the infamous man who persecutes Christians, we have Matthew—who everybody knows is a tax collector who steals money from people—we have prostitutes, and the list goes on of people we see in the Bible who followed Jesus when they were known to be outcasts in their society.

There they were, broken people labeled by the "righteous," following relentlessly after Jesus, and changing the world.

Before they knew Him, their lives didn't have much significance. Once they established a relationship with Him, the outpouring He gave them transformed into love, healing, and courage for others like no one had ever seen.

You see, it became less about who they were labeled as, and more about who they were to Jesus as friends working together as Guardians of His Kingdom.

Who are you? For some of us, it may be a matter of being known within our culture and society today. But, the true identity of who you are is *actually* made up by *whose* you are. You are God's.

Your identity is not made up of what you've done. It does not matter who you are or if you've been labeled as the scraps of society, because to the Father, you belong to Him, you are His child.

God can take anyone and equip them to do the extraordinary work of the kingdom of God. The Guardians of the Galaxy were all unlikely heroes who saved the galaxy; what makes you think you can't do the same?

God wants to use you, no matter what you have done.

Just like the Guardians of the Galaxy, just like the Apostles, you too can become a somebody.

A PLACE BEYOND THE PINES
(2012)

*After Jesus said this, he looked toward
heaven and prayed: "Father, the hour has
come. Glorify your Son, that your Son may
glorify you..." John 17:1 NIV*

Avery Cross is a new Police Officer in Schenectady,
New York. New on the job, Cross exhibits
distinguished pride, honor, and integrity. A true model
of what a Police Officer ought to be. He aims to do the
right thing in all he does (his reasons for doing so are
rooted in his internal conflict of a past altercation in
which he used deadly physical force), something his
current Police Department doesn't seem to understand.
After an unwarranted house search, his fellow cops
decide to sneak some seized cash to Cross for his own

spoils. Pressured to keep it, Cross does not sink to their level. Cross does the right thing and places the seized wad of cash on his Chief's desk. The Chief responds surprisingly and erratically, telling Cross "Get this [stuff] outta here." The person in the highest position in this Police Department, who is supposed to bring justice, has no interest in morality or dignity. The profession that is supposed to exemplify the most integrity does none of this, and it makes no sense to Cross.

Because of what Cross did, he is threatened by the Police Department. Threatened for being the good guy. He was a threat to them because he was doing the moral thing, and they were far from it. All he was trying to do was his best, applying values that any recruit would have learned at the academy. Instead, he faces the harsh reality of corruption and what it means to stand up for what is right.

After his conversation with the Chief, Avery's day tour ends. He gets into his car and begins driving home. As he drives, Deluca, a fellow cop who led the illegal house search, pulls him over and demands that Cross follow him. On the way, Cross realizes that Deluca is leading him to an isolated forest where there are no witnesses. In fear for his life, he intensely reverses his car and frantically speeds to his father's house.

He's in trouble and has nowhere else to go, except to his father.

Have you ever been in an environment where you felt you were the only one doing the right thing? That in the place you were in, you just couldn't see a shining light, you couldn't find any support? A place where anywhere you turned you encountered trouble? Sometimes, the world feels like that, more of the time than not, actually. Sometimes, the very situation we are in feels the same way. It feels like one dark place, where everyone is trying to strip you of your beliefs. It leaves us feeling lonely, unsupported, and unfulfilled.

When you have nowhere else to go and you feel like life is out of hand, go to your Father. The one who loves you and understands you more than anyone else. Jesus was about to face the darkest moment anyone would ever face, and He knew that the time had come. He was about to be stripped, alone, and unsupported. Jesus, in His perfect character, went to the Father in the midst of this horrific hour.

Know that you are not alone in this world. Though it may feel like darkness surrounds you, run to your Heavenly Father, and run to Him until you sense Him right by your side, supporting you, and lighting up the darkness that surrounds you.

ZOOTOPIA (2016)

When Joseph's brothers saw him coming,
they recognized him in the distance. As he
approached, they made plans to kill him.
"Here comes the dreamer!" they said.
"Come on, let's kill him and throw him into
one of these cisterns. We can tell our father,
'A wild animal has eaten him.' Then we'll
see what becomes of his dreams!"
Genesis 37:18-20 NLT

For all who have faced opposition while pursuing their dreams, this is for you. For all who have dreamed big but got shut down, it's not the end for you. Don't let dream killers get in your way.

Judy Hopps aspires to be a Police Officer. One problem…in the eyes of animals, she's a petite bunny. A bunny becoming a Police Officer is unheard of; it goes against every animal code. Her genetic makeup is gentle, fluffy, and small.

But she has the desire and the determination, and that's all that matters.

In pursuit of this dream, Hopps encounters animals who try to extinguish her dreams. As a *graduated* and *qualified* member of the Zootopia Police Academy, she gets demoted to parking duty, deals with harassment, and faces a threatened termination all because she is a bunny. But Judy Hopps doesn't give up. Despite all of the opposition, she keeps pursuing her passion for policing because it is what she wanted to do ever since she was a little hare.

In the Bible, Joseph had a dream. A dream that he would one day rule and that people would bow down to him. His brothers, after hearing of his dream, got so jealous they stripped him of his purple ornate robe, dropped him in a well, and sold him to slavery. Like Hopps, Joseph wasn't defeated. He endured the severity of slavehood, and a nasty and shameful accusation, but he didn't give up. Joseph eventually became ruler of Egypt.

If you are working toward achievement of a God-given dream, it is evident that you will face dream killers and foxes who want to scratch you. What do you do when this happens?

Be like Joseph and Hopps, please, don't stop pursuing your dream, don't give in to naysayers, and don't give up. To the world, you may be judged as a little bunny, but believe in yourself, and believe that God sees you as equipped, fierce, and qualified.

When you have a passion for something, go after it because *you* love it. No matter what people say, go after the dream that God has put in your heart. Please, if you've been constantly rejected for pursuing your dreams, keep going. Don't let what people say about your dream define you. And don't let their resistance defeat you.

THE ROOKIE (2002)

Abraham fell facedown; he laughed and said to himself, "Will a son be born to a man a hundred years old? Will Sarah bear a child at the age of ninety?" Genesis 17:17 NIV

What did you dream of becoming when you were younger? Do you think it's too late to achieve that dream? The reality is, it is never too late. Dream, no matter how old you are. God sees your desires and He supports you. He created you. He created those good desires in your heart.

Jim Morris has kids, a career, and a history of arm injuries. "The Rookie" is based on his true story, the story of a thirty-five year old who throws a 98 mph fastball, and who makes it to the MLB. No matter your age, it's never too late to dream.

Have you ever thought, 'When I was young I could have done this or when I was young I could have done that?' Why are you asking yourself these questions and living with such regret?

Why aren't you taking advantage of the day that is right before you? I think so many people make excuses. I'm too old, I can't do that. My mind doesn't work the way it used to, or I'm not strong enough. The reality is, you're not too old. The world has created a way of thinking that if you're a certain age, you're unable to do certain things. Don't think like that. These are just excuses that keep us from striving toward who we were meant to be. And if you don't feel qualified, He sees you as worthy of the training that you need in order to achieve those dreams.

Abraham was a one-hundred-year-old, God-fearing man. He laughed when God promised him that Sarah was going to have a child at the age of ninety. Sarah laughs as well (if we're being honest here, I might have, too). Even if we look at the science, we see that it's impossible for that to happen. But look what happens...Sarah bore

Isaac at ninety years old, just as promised. And even more important, Isaac becomes a part of Jesus' lineage. Nothing is impossible no matter your age. Even if your muscles deteriorate, your brain loses its cells, or your bones can't move—nothing is impossible with God.

I want you to start thinking like God: be crazy. The world says dreams end after you're 50, but what does God say? What limits are you putting on your age? God has none.

Even if it looks like something is over, don't lose hope. It's never too late to dream. If God has placed something in your heart that you desire, go for it no matter how old you are and no matter what messages are being spoken to you. Age is meaningless to God when He has a purpose for you. So live in the reality that anything can be accomplished no matter your age or situation. You did read that this movie is based on a TRUE STORY?

THE SANDLOT (1993)

*On hearing the Philistine's words, Saul
and all the Israelites were dismayed and
terrified. 1 Samuel 17:11 NIV*

His name is Smalls; he calls himself an Egghead. He thinks pretty lowly of himself. One summer, he meets new friends and gets to play baseball. *Batter up!* Smalls' friend, Ham, hits their last baseball up and over *the fence*. In his innocence, Smalls hurries to go and rescue it, but as we all know, his friends run up to that fence and yell, "NOO!" "Why?" one might ask. Well… "THE BEAST."

All of Smalls' friends generate fear of The Beast. One of the friends, Squints, tells the story of "The Legend of The Beast," of how "he grew big and he grew mean" through the evil power of his owner. Smalls is then afraid

43

of The Beast. The Beast seems big and scary, and he might devour someone.

A few days, a gut-busted baseball later, and desperate to play America's Pastime, Smalls saves the day with a ball he takes from his step dad's trophy room. He's up to bat...and hits his first homer over the fence. The ball he took from his step-dad's trophy room was a Babe Ruth signed baseball, and he needed to get that ball back.

As the movie progresses, Smalls and his friends use several gadgets to try to get that ball. The movie over-exaggerates The Beast and his size. It seems that the makers of the film wanted to show how big the kids thought The Beast really was and how desperate Smalls was to get that ball back.

For the first time, one of the friends, Benny the Jet Rodriguez, courageously hops the fence. We then see that The Beast is just a dog. Things aren't what they seem. Benny grabs the ball and hops back over the fence to freedom. The Beast clears the fence, chasing him all over town until ending up back at the baseball field. Benny and

Smalls attempt to return the dog to its owner. They are terrified. At the back steps, they converse with the owner, telling him the story. The conversation then leads to an unexpected reply, "Why didn't you just knock on the door? I would have gotten it for you." They could have just knocked on the door and the old man would have given them their baseball. How simple. They basically realized all of Benny's hard work and his sprint across town was for nothing. They could have just knocked on the door.

There is a correlation between "The Sandlot" and the story in the Bible about David and Goliath. In the midst of a battle, the Philistine's secret weapon, Goliath, confronts King Saul and asks for a fight. Saul and his men are terrified, just like Smalls and his friends. I'm sure that Saul and his men had heard of Goliath before. They themselves were terrified of the stories. Goliath was probably the tallest person they had ever seen. They are surprised when a small shepherd boy named David stands against Goliath and faces him. David defeats Goliath. David stands up to what is the embodiment of fear. This small person stands up to what people, even the King of Israel, were afraid of. We're all small. We all need to stand up to fear. Fear of that job interview, fear of the future, or anything that would keep us from moving forward.

Sometimes, we give in to fear and generate it ourselves from stories and experiences we hear. The reality is, fear is not something God made. It wasn't, "In the beginning God created man and he was terrified." No. It was, "because of the fall of man," that we have been vulnerable to these thoughts and generate fear.

In a way, we're all like Smalls. We're ordinary people who can be influenced and give in to fear. Will you stand up to what you're afraid of? Will you choose to not give in to fear? I challenge you today to identify The Beast in your life and face it, realizing that it may not be as big or as scary as you think. You can do it!

Because as The Great Bambino says to Benny the Jet, "Everybody gets one chance to do something great, most people never take the chance, either because they're too scared, or they don't recognize it when it spits on their shoes."

THE BABADOOK (2014)

*And being in anguish, he prayed more
earnestly, and his sweat was like drops of
blood falling to the ground. Luke 22:14 NIV*

Keep breathing. Put your seat back, sweetheart. Ten more minutes and we're there. I think it's gonna rain." These were the last words that Amelia remembers hearing from her husband, Oscar. She was in labor; he was in a hurry. That night spirals in her memory like a dark never-ending staircase. Every day she is surrounded by Samuel, her son, whom she loathes. Her emotions cloud her ability to emotionally care for her son. The black cloak, a rearview mirror, darkness, a beam of light...Oscar.

"Baba-dook-dook-dook"

Years passed. Samuel suggests to Amelia that they read a would-be children's book "Mister Babadook." They are both horrified of its contents. Samuel is a mere child and Amelia can't deal with her grief. The Babadook stalks her in her car's rear view mirror, the Babadook stalks her when she is alone, the Babadook stalks her son, the Babadook floods her everyday life. Mister Babadook somehow reminds her of Oscar.

"As soon as anyone mentions Oscar, you can't cope."

There is one scene where Amelia and Samuel are in a grocery store. Samuel is showing a magic trick to a little girl in the store. Amelia excuses her son, and the little girl's mother replies by saying they're going to see her daddy. To which Samuel reacts: "My dad is in the cemetery, he got killed driving mum to the hospital to have me." Amelia interrupts Samuel and cannot deal with the conversation. The soda bottle has been shaken and is ready to pop. Mister Babadook gets bigger and bigger as Amelia shoves her pain down further and further.

Pain can sometimes go so deep that everywhere we turn, we are reminded of the experience(s) that haunt(s) us. That memory for Amelia distorted the relationship with her son—to the point of not even celebrating her son's birthday. To the point of wanting Samuel dead because the pain was associated with her pregnancy. Her pain had blinded her.

At a crucial point, when she had enough, Amelia confronts the Babadook. She sees her husband and she relives his last moments. Her trauma, her pain, her fear— she relentlessly takes her anguish out on the Babadook who in return shrieks and shrivels its way down, down, down into the basement behind locked doors. The Babadook, the pain, the horror—we see it diminish as Amelia takes control and finally…there is peace. Finally, she can look at her son and celebrate his life.

You can't just shake it off and move forward when everywhere you look, there's the pain or reminder of that person or thing. Amelia witnessed the gruesome death of her husband in the midst of her pregnant labor. Her son, the lights, a black coat, lovers kissing, a fender bender... she couldn't escape it.

Do you feel like Amelia? Does your pain, loss, tragedy influence your daily experiences?

Dealing with your pain is a very scary thing. Although, it becomes more bearable with Jesus at your side.

If we believe that He came to give abundant life, we must apply this biblical truth to our own lives. When we are confronted with trauma, with pain, with any kind of hardship, stuffing it down will only produce death, a false sense of reality, and/or destruction. If you allow Jesus and people who have the awareness to grieve with you and lead you toward Jesus, into these painful places, eventually, the trauma, the pain, the horror will lose its terrifying grip on your life. And just like Amelia, you will have control over your pain rather than it having control over you.

THE BABADOOK

What do you do? What do you do when you don't know what else to do? When your pain begins to haunt you?

Let Jesus into your pain, into your loss, into your fear, into your taunting anxieties. He wants to wrap you in His arms and gently untwist what has been twisted, and if you allow yourself to open up to Him in your pain, He will sing you a song of healing. Sit with Jesus, let Him love you right where you are. If that painful thing seems like a lot to deal with, just know that you have God—bigger than tragedy itself—and people (generally, most of you have safe ones) at your side who can walk in this with you.

Is there something in your life that you feel is too painful to revisit? The encouragement today is that it is very possible to revisit it, with Jesus. No matter how painful, you can grieve your pain, grieve your losses with Jesus at your side. God will hold you to His chest. Cry with Him, let Him nurture and care for your tired heart.

If there is anyone who understands pain, trauma, tragedy— it's Jesus. If you do this, if you allow Him into those scary places, He will give you peace.

INSIDE OUT (2015)

*Laughter can conceal a heavy heart, but
when the laughter ends, the grief remains.*
Proverbs 14:13 NLT

Why are people so bad at being sad?

Joy and Sadness clash in our daily lives. "Inside
Out" follows the life of a teen named Riley, whose
emotions conflict with each other within the confines of
her psyche. Joy likes to monopolize Riley's life, never
giving Riley a chance to experience Sadness. Why?
Because at the heart of it, Joy doesn't understand Sadness.

In the beginning of the film, we see that Riley's
life drastically changes when she begins to pack up the
wonderful experiences she once shared with her family,
friends, and hockey team, as she must move halfway

across the country from Minnesota to San Francisco. Deep down, she misses it all, she is tragically saddened and begins to battle with expressing these feelings. Riley believes that it is not beneficial for her family to show her true emotions, thinking that it is her responsibility to be the family's pillar of strength.

There are times when we go to the same extremes, trying to hide our pain and act as if everything is fine. There's no set answer for why we do this, but I think we can all agree that it's not healthy or genuine. God does not call us to be fake. He does not call us to be fake with Him, and He does not call us to be fake with other people.

Fake it till you make it, right? Or better yet just don't talk about sad stuff at all. Just put on a smile and pretend that everything is dandy. It seems like this is an easy thing to do. Show the bright colors—all the happy ones. But are these the only colors out there?

It's actually okay to show the darker colors if you're feeling that way (Psalm 51:17). Be honest with God and yourself—and when you find someone that is trustworthy, be honest with them too. Being real, being genuine, is the only way to discover true intimacy and fulfillment in our relationships with God and people. No need to be afraid.

God knows what you are going through; there is no reason to hide your emotions.

Be genuine with how you feel; He can handle it. It's okay to cry.

Don't sugarcoat your pain. When you are hurt it's okay to express all of your hurt to God. Bring it all to Him with no strings attached. What I mean is, if you are hurt about something, don't end the sentence with a "but." It just doesn't work like that. Validate your pain, He does. Blaming yourself for someone else hurting you doesn't work either. If you have deep hurt in your life, bring it all to God. Let the tears flow and don't put up a dam.

Deal with the pain in your life. Don't shove it down and act as if everything is okay, if you keep doing that it will pop back up again sooner or later and sometimes in ways we don't like nor can we control. God understands what you're going through. Walk through the processes of loss with Him and walk through the joys of life with Him. God sees all things, He is El Roi (Gen 16:13). Don't worry—God is not out to get you. He is gentle and compassionate.

Sometimes life is not all about pulling yourself up from the bootstraps and moving forward. Sometimes it's good to be sad!

Accepting your sadness can also help you to love others as well. If you know how to grieve, you can properly grieve with people. If someone approaches you and wants to share their deep pain, are you going to respond like Joy or Sadness? The most loving thing would be to meet them where they are; weep with those who weep, have we forgotten that?

God cares about your emotions. Don't sugar coat them. He wants your whole heart, not one part of your heart. So be real with Him and be real with yourself.

THE REVENANT (2015)

...And let us run with perseverance the race
marked out for us, fixing our eyes on Jesus,
the pioneer and perfecter of faith...
Hebrews 12:1-2 NIV

It was cold but they were warm. Huddled together like peas in a pod, mother, father, and son, they would never be left astray.

Life was peaceful for a short moment, but tragedy strikes as Hugh Glass' wife dies, and Hawk, his son, becomes thrust into maturity in his young age.

And if that weren't enough, Hugh is attacked by a burly brown bear, leaving him at the cusp of death. Hugh survives, but living through such an attack seems colder than death.

His strenuous wheezing clouds the air. Fitzgerald—that name keeps Hugh alive. Fitzgerald, that slimy, incompetent, irrational wretch had murdered Hawk and attempted to bury Hugh alive. Hugh's mouth began foaming, barely breathing, he kept gnawing at the soil, screaming, wondering if someone would hear his cry.

"All I had was my boy and he took him from me, you understand?"

Life had left Hugh naked—stripped of all that he loved. His manhood had been raped, and Fitzgerald's betrayal was Hugh's downfall. Somehow Hugh clawed fingernail by fingernail through the icy dirt, stumbling, trying to survive. Surviving in the name of his son, clinging to life with the hope of destroying the man who took his offspring.

Sometimes, life leaves us feeling stripped of everything. You work so hard in your profession, yet you get laid off. You honor your spouse, they end up leaving. You pursue your dreams, yet they are crushed. Or, all of that happens to you one by one and then loved ones tragically die. Somehow, you keep surviving. I think we can learn from Hugh's life. He had been through death, yet he kept going, thinking of one day seeing his wife and his son again. He keeps propelling himself forward with the motivation of one thing, survival.

A lot of people think this movie drags on and is slow-paced. It's a long movie, but I think it paints a picture of how life was going for Hugh. And a lot of times in life, it's like you're moving slowly or barely at all.

I am sure that Hugh Glass wanted to quit many times on his trek. He was faced with so much adversity. His wife dies, his son dies, and he himself gets mauled by a bear, falls off a cliff, and is pulled along by rapids. Hugh withstands all of his tragedies; he keeps going...he keeps breathing.

No matter where you are, God is right by your side. And as you keep running the race (you may have many cuts and bruises from it and maybe only able to crawl through this marathon of life), keep going, look to Jesus, just like how Hugh kept going, through the motivation he finds in the memories of his wife and son. It will be tough. I'm not going to say that it's going to be an easy journey but it will be worth it.

We can learn something when it comes to persevering. When you are feeling like you are on a frozen hill in subzero temperatures with no sun on the horizon, pursue Jesus with all that you have. Keep going and never give up.

No matter where you are, no matter what you're going through, God is constant. If you feel like the journey you're on won't end and there is no sigh of relief at the end, God will be with you. Not only is He with you, but He knows what it is like to suffer intensely, to be lashed with stabbing whips, forced to hold his body up with a slab of extremely heavy and awkwardly shaped wood on his back, while being pushed to keep on walking. When we feel like Jesus did, like Hugh, it is these moments when we need Him to carry us, to be our strength to keep going. It's when we're at our weakest moments, that Christ's power rests on us. He promises to never leave you or forsake you in the midst of this. Don't give up. Keep running this race. Look at the adversity that Jesus faced while on this earth and keep running, walking, crawling. Don't let anything tear you down on this journey. Keep fighting and keep going. Embrace the King in the struggle. Don't give up. He will be your reward in the middle of it all, if you just keep your eyes on Him.

GROUNDHOG DAY (1993)

*See! The winter is past; the rains are over
and gone. Flowers appear on the earth; the
season of singing has come, the cooing of
doves is heard in our land.
Song of Solomon 2:11-12 NIV*

Wouldn't it be awesome if we did not have to endure the wintery season and just had a lifetime of beautiful sunshine? I bet that is what heaven is like (well maybe for some; some of us like the snow).

There's no denying how magical winter can be: snow, silent nights, and hot cocoa. There is also another side to winter—mundane, bitter, freezing, and depressing.

Sometimes, we may feel as if we are stuck in a season of life that is like a never-ending winter. A season in which every day just feels the same: empty, going through the motions, like it won't be ending anytime soon—or ever. It's in these moments when seeking God is most crucial.

When you're in the middle of a mundane season like this, know that God is doing something special in the ordinary. Even if every step you take feels cold, depressing, and hollow, embrace God in your winter. If you embrace Him, He will bring you into the next season stronger than ever before.

Phil Connors is a weatherman assigned to report on Groundhog Punxsutawney Phil's major decision regarding the change of winter into spring. Phil the reporter (not the groundhog) is cold and salty. His attitude matches that of the winter season. Phil half-heartedly finishes his day in despair that there would be a lovely six more weeks of winter, and goes to sleep in his hotel bed. He wakes up...to the same exact day, again, and again, and again....

Phil is peeved at the fact that he is to endure the monotonous ritual of literally reliving the same day in Nowheres-ville, Pennsylvania. Although sick with the mundane, his interest is peaked as he begins to take notice of Rita, his coworker on the Groundhog Day Report. This interest in Rita blossoms into love. Rita is a precious one…her name even means "pearl."

"What I really want is someone like you."

There are certain days that Rita rejects Phil, but he still continues to pursue her. It's because of Phil's love for Rita that he is motivated to live this revolving door cycle of the same day every single day. Phil's love for Rita keeps him going through the mundane. Phil wants more of Rita and wants to win her over with his heart. It's because of his love for her, that he realizes he could use the constant repetition of days for the development of his cold heart to grow and learn to become a warmer person.

Your love and pursuit for Jesus will sustain you through the ordinary and plain.

So what do you do if you feel like you're stuck in a cold season that brings no flowers? Or a bitter season that contains no joy? You pursue Jesus. God will always meet you right where you are. Keep desiring God no matter what the circumstance. Continue to worship Him in the middle of the season in which you can't see in front of you because of the cold, wet, unwanted fog. Keep your eyes on the Sun (Son.. get it?.. that was a pun). If you are able to press into Him in the midst of the wintery season, your character, your ability to persevere, will be stronger than ever before. It may take much blood, sweat, and tears, but keep your eyes on the prize; the result will be well worth it, no matter how long your 'groundhog' says winter will last.

On a side note, I think we can learn from groundhogs. They hibernate an average of around three months. In frigid temperatures, they find a safe place where they can stay warm and rest. The safe place for you is found in Jesus, and however long this season goes on for, God is willing to be with you through it all. Even if it feels tough and situations feel like they are against you, rest in Jesus.

It's as simple as meditating on all things Him while driving to that job you hate but currently can't quit because of finances, working through relationship struggles, folding laundry while your kids bounce around the house making more of a mess, humming a worship song in bed, or meditating on God's word while working out. Your God is bigger than the winter season, and because you have Him, you too, can rise above it and not be frozen by its wintery seasonal effects.

FROZEN (2013)

When Simon Peter saw this, he fell at Jesus'
knees and said, "Go away from me, Lord; I
am a sinful man!" Luke 5:8 NIV

♪

Do you want to fish for men? Come out and
follow me. ♪

In Frozen we are introduced to two sisters, Elsa
and Anna. Elsa is different; she has special ice powers.
Anna just wants to play with her big sister. One day
while playing, Elsa (using her powers to create a winter
wonderland) can't catch up with how fast Anna is
playing, so Elsa, in a hurry to catch up with her sister,
slips and accidentally hits Anna in the head with her ice
powers. Like most of us know, Elsa had no interest in
ever hurting Anna again so she locks herself in her room
and her childhood passes by behind that closed door.

Shame shackles Elsa into feeling extreme guilt for hurting her sister, letting the accident define her and her powers. She believes herself to be a monster unworthy of affection, which is why she isolates herself from Anna so that she could never hurt her sister again.

But Anna does not relent in pursuit of rekindling their bond of sisterhood as she knocks, sings, and talks to Elsa through her bedroom door. Anna continues this ritual for years, pleading with Elsa to join her in building a snowman, a pastime they once partook in.

"Go away Anna."

We do this with God. God wants to take us places, spend time just doing life together, but unfortunately because of our shame, we fail to recognize that we are forgiven and able to do so. Elsa became like a turtle, instead of trusting herself, showing the beauty of her ice powers, she stayed in her rock solid shell, ashamed, fearful, alone, and afraid.

"Only an act of true love can thaw a frozen heart."

In the midst of keeping her sister out, yet again, Elsa accidentally freezes most of Arendelle, and casts ice crystals into Anna's heart. She has basically killed her own sister. In one of the final scenes, Anna uses her last moments before she is fully frozen to sacrifice her life to protect Elsa from an oncoming attacker. How ironic. It is this final scene that I truly believe Elsa let go of shame. She realizes that her sister Anna has an undying love for her. The healing that came from Anna's sacrifice is a glimpse of what Jesus has done for us. The key to breaking free from this shame is to daily focus on the sacrifice that Jesus made for us.

Even if we might know that Jesus sacrificed himself for us, we get frozen sometimes; we still carry shame and guilt for the things we have done, not letting Jesus take care of our brokenness.

Have you done something in your life which you feel you can't be forgiven for? Do you feel like Elsa? Jesus is knocking on your door, singing, and wanting to be with you— to show you beauty, to dethaw what has been frozen. Will you open the door to Him?

Love is the biggest destroyer of shame. The enemy throws shame at us if we do something wrong because the enemy wants us to believe that the cross is not enough. The reality is that God wants to be with you, just as you are, a broken person, in need of a *friend*.

Ask God to reveal if there is anything He wants to set you free from. There is no issue too big for Him. Don't be isolated by the lies that keep your door closed, listen to His knock, experience His relentless love, grace, and freedom. Let your shame go. Let it go.

RATATOUILLE (2007)

"No one lights a lamp and then hides it or puts it under a basket. Instead, a lamp is placed on a stand, where its light can be seen by all who enter the house…"
Luke 11:33 NLT

When you are gifted at something, you let it shine. No matter who you are or where you come from, don't be ashamed of your talents. If you're gifted in a certain area, use that gift wonderfully.

Remy the Rat, yes a rat, was born with a talent to cook and not just to cook, but to craft gourmet French cuisine. A rodent connoisseur with exquisite taste, Remy, subject by his dad to eat garbage food and do the menial tasks given to him, is so passionate about pursuing his cooking that he does whatever it takes.

There, in the middle of his search for direction toward his dream and to satisfy the driving urge to indulge his senses, was the beautifully lit Gusteau's sign overlooking the Paris skyline. Gusteau's, a former five star restaurant was owned by the late Auguste Gusteau who truly believed that "Anyone can cook." It is this phrase that drives Remy toward becoming a chef. His heart, his senses, his passion could not stop him from pursuing this dream.

While Remy peers through the top window of Gusteau's overlooking the kitchen's sights, sounds, and smells, he encounters his worst nightmare—someone is ruining the soup! Overwhelmed, his body uncontrollably falls through the window landing him in paradise... The Kitchen.

A rat in a kitchen?! Alone, that is disgraceful, but what would they say if they saw a rat cook?? So he hides himself under Linguini's tall white chef hat. Linguini is the man ruining the soup. We would think that Linguini would know how to cook because he is kin to the late Gusteau, but it surely doesn't work like that in this movie. Sometimes the greatest gifts are found in the most unexpected places, or in this case a vermin.

Remy had to hide himself, because if the world knew he could cook, there would be dire consequences…or at least this is what he thought.

So this cycle of hiding himself under Linguini's hat went on for Remy. He would dodge the sight of any person who might see him. He did this for quite a while. And yes, for those who haven't seen this Disney food-loving, lip-licking blockbuster, Linguini knew Remy was under there; they had become friends over the initial fact that Remy made Linguini look good in the kitchen.

Anton Ego, the nationally-feared food critic, showed up at Gusteau's one evening. He had ordered Remy's special, Ratatouille. This time though, Remy couldn't hide himself. The dish revelled Ego, and he demanded to see the Chef. Remy was finally unveiled, and to the most revered critic at that. Ego was astonished…

Imagine the dramatic pause, the shock that occurred here. Ego was so utterly impressed with this delectable dish, he completely disregards the fact that Remy is a rat, and praises him for his extraordinary talent in the kitchen.

The biggest message in this film: don't hide your gifts. I think as humans, we have disregarded what we can actually accomplish in life and have let ourselves, or at least the talents we've been gifted with, to take the form of a rat, something that is small, undesirable, and doesn't want to be seen by people. The lesson here is to show yourself to the world with the gifts God has given you, and let them shine bright, without shame.

Why are you hiding your light from the world, and from those around you? Is it because if people see that you are truly something wonderful, they might reject you? You are not a rat. You are a child of God, so shine your light and don't hide under a Chef's hat. Display that rich, stunning goodness (you, your gifts and talents) that you were made to shine on this world. What people say about you or your talent doesn't matter. Don't let critics stop you from what you know is innately inside of you and has been created to spill out. It doesn't matter what you look like, what you've done, or what people expect of you.

I want to encourage you to have more confidence in yourself, and to foster the gifts you've been given. Take the next step and work toward the display of that light. You were made to let those gifts shine, to steward those things that make you uniquely you. Know with confidence, that as you proceed forward, God is supporting your every move. Don't allow yourself to be a rat that hides under the Chef's hat. Now go, shine that light on the world, and shine it brightly. The world is waiting.

ANT-MAN (2015)

Then I heard the voice of the Lord saying,
"Whom shall I send? And who will go for
us?" And I said, "Here am I. Send me!"
Isaiah 6:8 NIV

Scott Lang is a full-time stealing specialist…who basically gets caught and sent to prison. After serving his sentence, Scott attempts to build a stronger relationship with his young daughter. He gets a job at Baskin Robbins, but that doesn't last. So, Scott returns to what he knows best: professional thievery. Not long after, he ends up back in the slammer.

Through the use of a small herd of ants, Hank Pym, retired CEO of PYM Technologies, presents Scott with a superhero suit and a way out of his sentence. Hank gives

Scott a chance at redemption, and a chance at freedom. All he needs to do is 'be' the Ant-Man.

Hank Pym was impressed with Scott's criminal expertise and sought his help in order to stop the Yellow Jacket from wreaking havoc on the world. When Hank presents this case to Scott, what is his reply? "I think our first move should be calling the Avengers." Instead of having confidence in himself, Scott believes Marvel's greatest heroes are better suited. He even wonders if Pym's ants could do the job for him. Really deep down, Scott doesn't believe he is good enough.

Hank Pym is basically giving Scott the Ant-Man suit. Hank believes in Scott, in his skill and in his ability. The message being sent to Scott is, "I need you to be in the game. No more sitting on the sidelines; it's time for you to jump in and do this thing."

Scott feels unqualified, but because Hank believes in him, he is able to put on the suit and be the Ant-Man.

In the movie, Scott says basically the same thing that Isaiah from the Bible did: "'Woe to me!' I cried. 'I am ruined! For I am a man of unclean lips, and I live among a people of unclean lips, and my eyes have seen the King, the LORD Almighty.'" But then a seraphim flies and puts a burning coal on his tongue and tells Isaiah that his sins are forgiven. Um what?! Isaiah goes from feeling like he can't do it, to someone who is empowered by God and sent on a mission to proclaim God's word. His cry goes from "I am ruined" to "Here am I send me" (Isaiah 6:5-8).

How would you respond to being called to change the world? Picture Jesus as Hank Pym and yourself as Scott. Jesus is handing you a superhero suit and He's asking you to put it on, to bring light to the dark places, to be that world changing superhero. Will you answer the call and bring light to this world in the details of your daily life? In the lunchroom with your coworkers? Will you stand up for what is honorable in His eyes?

God asks you these questions, and you can answer them every single day. God asks you because you are just as good as the Avengers. Because He believes YOU can bring revival, YOU can bring light and life to all that you interact with daily. Just like Scott Lang, a thief, *chosen* by Hank Pym, you're just as qualified, skilled, and significant as those who have already brought revival and world change.

I challenge you today to take the opportunity and learn from the best hero ever, Jesus. You can do this! Put on that suit and go be a hero for God!

SPIDER-MAN HOMECOMING (2017)

See what kind of love the Father has given to us, that we should be called children of God; and so we are...1 John 3:1 ESV

Peter Parker desperately needs a dad. With only Aunt May in the picture, even just a father figure would have sufficed.

Peter is all about aiming to prove himself, and not-always-flawlessly strives to show the world that he can be an amazing superhero despite being a teen. Even though he is passionate, what's his motive for trying to prove himself? For someone to acknowledge and help cultivate his sense of worth.

JESUS LOVES MOVIES

There's a desperate need in all of us for the Father's love.

I started to cry as I watched this film for the first time. Peter had witnessed so much loss in the span of his life. He isn't just a teenager, he is a teenager with a hopeless need for guidance.

Peter works so hard to prove that he can be the Spider-Man. Beneath this is a cry for someone to be proud of him. Luckily, Tony Stark comes into the picture. Tony Stark, of all people, is the one to show Peter the fatherly love he so desires. But not necessarily in the way he expects.

Peter needs to understand his worth as a man before becoming the Spider-Man. Tony tells Peter: "If you're nothing without the suit, then you shouldn't have it." Tony's words fall on stubborn ears because Peter is so set on being the best superhero out there.

Finally, Stark's words of wisdom resonate with Peter as he realizes it's not about becoming the Spider-Man, but it was always about Peter becoming Peter. He needs someone who will accept him and love him the way he was, not solely for his Spidey abilities. Peter needs Tony, and Tony's acceptance of Peter? It was never about his performance. Tony understood Peter, because he had his own father-induced scars.

You don't need to prove yourself to God, and because of this, you don't need to prove yourself to others. You are already loved. Abba doesn't want you to strive to impress Him. He just wants you to be you. When we strive to be or do more than who we are, we miss the point. Why strive, when you are already His child? When you are already on His team?

God is your Father, your potter, and the One who shapes you. He makes you into who you were meant to be. God wants you to have a sense of belonging, acceptance, and love, without the need to perform. He is interested in who you are first and foremost, there's no need to strive.

MEAN GIRLS (2004)

Then Jesus said to his disciples, "If anyone
would come after me, let him deny himself
and take up his cross and follow me..."
Matthew 16:24 ESV

I misinterpreted this verse from Matthew when I first became a Christian. For quite a while, I thought God was telling me to forget who He made me to be and be someone I wasn't. I shut off 'fun' in my life and replaced it with what I thought God wanted for me in life. I was like a robot who followed God without a heart, obeying every order in the Bible—literally. I even took the fun out of strict fundamentalism.

Do you ever just want to fit in? Do you ever just want to be accepted by people? It's natural to want to be liked. The problem arises, though, when we give up who we really are in order to gain friends. Sometimes we lose who we are in the process, just to make friends, and we become someone we are not.

"He was so cute."

It's math class and Cady Heron is a wiz. That cute guy, Aaron Samuels is sitting in front of her. In order to muster up a conversation, she pretends that she is terrible at the math and asks him for help. She actually flunks a test in order to get his math-tutoring attention.

Cady becomes someone she's not in order for a guy to like her.

Jesus calls us to deny ourselves, but that doesn't mean becoming someone we're not so that Jesus can embrace us. God is not about that. He has made you to be unique! Don't lose yourself literally by shutting off the things that make you, you, just to please Him. If you think this is what He is like, you've got the wrong image of the Father.

Be authentic.

Don't believe the lie. The lie that you have to fit in with everyone and become like everyone. The truth is you are accepted by God. God has created you. You! The very you that loves to eat good food, enjoy the outdoors, go shopping, watch movies, write, read, play sports, play video games, etc. The activities you like to do are the things that make you, you! The God of the Universe actually cares about you, and He was the one who placed those amazing, detailed desires in your heart! You don't have to perform for God's acceptance. You are already accepted. He ain't no Regina George!

This is freedom! God calls us into this freedom. HE accepts you into His family. Everyone is accepted, all you have to do is follow Him and be YOU. What makes you, uniquely you is wonderful in God's sight. Choose to be the way God created you; don't be somebody else. God accepts all of you. Just *go* to Him. That's right, "You go, Glenn Coco!"

WONDER WOMAN (2017)

*She is clothed with strength and dignity; she
can laugh at the days to come.
Proverbs 31:25 NIV*

Strength and dignity…two of the strongest traits of
the Amazons—who are part of an ancient Greek
world made of only females, a world in which women
run society and influence the heart of man.

Since the day she was born, Diana was destined to
kill Ares—who we could basically equate to Satan. You
see at the time, Diana didn't know she had it in her. Her
purpose, her drive, innately, she was the one. Diana was
"The God Killer," the only one who could defeat Ares
himself; the one who would incite all people to do evil
things. As we see in the film, Diana is stronger and more
powerful than countless men. Her adventurous childhood

was spent training with the strongest Amazon warrior, Antiope. After centuries of intense battlefront training, Diana's time comes to end Ares.

Fast forward… to keep with the movie theme, pretend I am telling you to press fast forward on your remote.

There Diana was, sitting in the bar. Steve Trevor and his motley gang were showing Diana who he would recruit for his squad to enter battle. Diana, determined to find Ares, told the gang that she was coming with them to war. Charlie, Steve's washed-up war bud, responded by saying: "Listen sweetheart, I'm not going to get myself killed helping a wee lassie out of a ditch." This came from the mouth of a cowardly man who couldn't even shoot a bullet from his rifle.

I think this speaks to a lot of what is going on in our present day.

Unfortunately, women have been treated as less than men since the beginning of time. This is pure evil. The serpent attacks a woman first, why? Not because women are more susceptible to attack but because the enemy was trying to instill oppression in women since the beginning, preventing them to be truly who they are meant to be.

"Diana!" "I can't let you do this."

Throughout the film, Diana is discouraged from doing what her heart is telling her to do, what she WAS MADE FOR. She is constantly being shut down, primarily because she is a woman and she is viewed as WEAK. Women, please, don't let people stop you from achieving what you are made to do.

There's a scene when Steve takes Diana to "No Man's Land," a battle zone that no man has crossed before. Steve's incessant voice of worry reveals that he thinks Diana is not capable of crossing such a dangerous battleground, "how can a woman cross what men have never crossed?" Diana, proves him wrong. It's one of the most powerful scenes in the movie because Diana crosses that zone. Facing heavy fire, still she moves forward.

She still moves forward. Despite the heavy fire.

Women, when a man, media, society, the world, infers that you can't do something, it means nothing in comparison to what God says. You may even face attack when you are on that journey, but don't give up, stay equipped and strong. Keep moving forward. Know that the most POWERFUL One is fighting for you, honors you, and treasures you.

God is not concerned about gender when it comes to getting a job done.

If it weren't for women, Jesus wouldn't have the story he has today. Women were the first witnesses of Jesus' resurrection, and uh…Mary?

The world needs women operating in their fullness. They are an important part of God's image. That's kind of a big deal. Unfortunately I am speaking to the people that fail to recognize this. Please, rid yourself of the belief, worldview, what have you, that women are weak, fragile, and less than men. This goes against the heart of

God, the ultimate POWER, the ultimate RULER. To all women who have felt the effects of our flawed emotional, spiritual, economic, cultural, structural system, I am sorry. On behalf of all men, I deeply apologize. You were never meant to be pushed down. In the beginning, God made male AND female in His image. If we push others down, if we discourage them, we are pushing the very image of God down with them.

Men, it's time to repent on behalf of yourself and all men. Repent on stopping women from achieving their purpose because you think they're too weak. With your help, men, we can make a great change and love women the way they were meant to be loved. So all lady warriors, gear up and fight. Men, I ask you to be like Jesus, to support your sisters to the best of your ability, and provide them with the opportunity to empower themselves to be the best they can be.

To those who have been oppressed in any way, arise. It's time to stand up. It's time to be defined by the Father's view of you despite this oppression.

Women, when the battle comes, will you stand strong? Will you know who you are, a child of God and stand strong in the face of adversity?

Be strong and courageous. You have Jesus, He is your Trainer, He believes in you, He desires to train you into your destiny, every single day. He has equipped you with great armor to stand courageously, defend properly, and fight when the battle rages. Your responsibility is to never give the enemy a foothold in your life. Women, your fight for maintaining your God-given identity is a spiritual fight. Your Warrior Jesus, is the One who was victorious in death and trains you to fight, God is FOR you.

One of Christ's purposes was to bring an end to the enemy and his hold on our lives. Dream big and take back that land! Go where no man has gone before.

HACKSAW RIDGE (2016)

"...The LORD does not look at the things people look at. People look at the outward appearance, but the LORD looks at the heart." 1 Samuel 16:7 NIV

Desmond Doss is a young Christian man from Lynchburg, Virginia who has a conviction to never touch a gun. Yet he desires to serve as a Combat Medic in the Army during World War II.

During bootcamp, Desmonds' fellow comrades torment him nearly to death. They dislike his faith and his refusal to use a gun, as did his leaders in authority. Like anyone might, they have extreme doubts that he will be able to sustain battle conditions without firing a weapon, let alone save them from the hand of enemy forces. These are just some of the thoughts of Desmond

Doss' associate soldiers: "He's just a skinny kid and a wimp who doesn't want to touch a gun. How is he going to save my life?"

Battle Location: Island of Okinawa, Hacksaw Ridge

Enemy Forces: Japanese

Classification: Known as one of the bloodiest events on the Pacific theater during WWII.

Time seemed to stop in its tracks as Doss and his Infantry Company passed by the war stricken and shell shocked American soldiers returning to base from Hacksaw Ridge. Stretcher bearers carrying dead and deformed bodies of the soldiers that had gone before them passed by the advancing troop, and the faces of those living exhibited mental and physical haunting. The seed sank deeper for Desmond, cultivating an even more intense desire to save his yet-to-be-fallen soldiers. Despite the severity of battle conditions, the company moved forward and made the ascent to the top of Hacksaw Ridge.

The battle was more devastating than expected, and Doss' infantry is forced to retreat. All soldiers who were able made it back to the base camp, except for Doss. He stayed on the Ridge, all alone, searching for soldiers to save. He keeps praying "Lord help me get one more." And when he finds them, he uses a rope and shimmies them down to the bottom of the Ridge, where his fellow comrades collect and send them to the medic tent. Desmond truly relies on God's strength to bring wounded soldiers to safety.

His fellow soldiers in safety at the camp receive notice that Desmond is all alone, and he is the one saving the lives of the soldiers being shimmied down. They are all dumbfounded and feel convicted that what they once said about him was false.

Doss proves all of them wrong. During horrific and violent frontline conditions, Doss becomes the driving force which motivates his fellow soldiers to keep fighting.

After Desmond rescues a record of 75 soldiers on Hacksaw Ridge that day, his Captain (who had been having a difficult time with him throughout boot camp), deeply apologizes to Doss for underestimating him. All he saw was a skinny kid.

Have you ever been quickly judged by someone? Have you ever felt like all people see is your outward appearance? All Doss' comrades saw was his physical appearance, and they didn't see the force behind his bravery.

Do you ever feel like your identity is under attack from those around you?

It's not about proving yourself to others either: it's about realizing that you're much more than what people say.

It's about what God says about you. That's the most important thing. You know what He sees? God sees much more than what people see—God sees your heart, a soldier's heart. That was all that Desmond needed, and he found strength in God in the most horrific of circumstances. When the soldiers in his own company were harassing him or when all sources of weapons were against him, he did not waver in who he was, which enabled him to save 75 lives.

Will you listen to what God says about you first and foremost? If those who are supposed to support you stand against you and life feels like a battle in which your identity feels under attack, will you stick to your guns and know that you are God's child? God never underestimates you, He always sees you for who you truly are, His brave child.

SPLIT (2017)

*Then Peter remembered the word Jesus had
spoken: "Before the rooster crows, you will
disown me three times." And he went outside
and wept bitterly. Matthew 26:75 NIV*

Teenager Casey Cooke goes to her friend's party at
a restaurant. Claire invited everyone in art class,
so she couldn't leave out Casey. Claire's dad ends up
taking Casey home, too, because she can't find a ride. As
Claire's father stuffs the party gifts and leftovers into the
trunk, the girls hop into the car. A victim of PTSD, Casey
is frozen with fear and unable to defend her friends or
herself as she realizes Claire's father has been attacked
by their soon-to-be abductor. Casey turns her head to face
the driver's seat, and there he is, Kevin Wendell Crumb.

"Kevin Wendell Crumb you made a mess."

In the midst of trying to survive, Casey finds out that if she says his full name, he is triggered back to the memory of where his childhood abuse began: hiding under his bed, awaiting his mother's punishment for making a mess. "Kevin Wendell Crumb!!!!" His name is being violently screamed—we all know what happens next.

In the Bible, there was something that triggered Peter back to a traumatic memory. The natural noise of a rooster reminded him of his own betrayal of his dear, blameless friend who had been recently crucified. The gospel says that Jesus was about to die when He told Peter that Peter would deny Him three times before the rooster crowed. Peter thought he was never going to see Jesus again (Imagine that. Your special, sweet friend, is about to die, and you basically disown them before their death). Peter probably thought that this conversation would be the last memory he would have of Jesus. This was truly traumatic.

There might be something that triggers a memory for you that you constantly think about, and all it does is bring you guilt, loss, or pain. The reality is, Jesus can restore you. Are you willing to bring that memory to Him and let Him heal you?

He did that for Peter. Jesus came back to life, and Peter was able to reunite in confession and healing with his Friend. This is a direct example of Jesus restoring someone who has been emotionally and psychologically heartbroken.

About a year ago, I was in New York City giving meals out to people struggling with homelessness, and I ran out of meals. I began talking to a young red headed veteran who was homeless and told him I had just run out of food. He told me it was fine. I asked him how he was doing, and he told me that he had Post Traumatic Stress Disorder. His PTSD was associated with a memory in which one of his fellow soldiers purposely stepped right in front of him as a grenade launcher was shot. His friend died from the wounds but this veteran lived. The guilt he felt was evident to me. I asked him if he wanted to pray and bring Jesus into that memory. He agreed.

I simply prayed, "Jesus would you reveal yourself in this memory."

As we prayed, He pictured Jesus healing his friend's wounds and bringing him to heaven where he had no more pain. The veteran also heard a word from God that it wasn't his fault and began to weep. On top of that, one bystander bought fresh hot food for him to eat.

You see, God wants to comfort you and wrap you in His arms. He cares about your memories and wants to restore them, no matter how big or small. Let Jesus reveal Himself to you in your memories. Let Jesus comfort you in your pain. Just invite Him in, ask Him where He was in those memories, and see what happens.

MONSTERS INCORPORATED (2001)

*...Like a shepherd, he will care for his flock,
gathering the lambs in his arms, hugging
them as he carries them, leading the nursing
ewes to good pasture. Isaiah 40:9-11 MSG*

Feeling safe around someone is a sign of precious trust. The problem with trust is that when broken, it brings pain and fear. The truth is, re-establishing that bond is difficult.

Sully is a valued employee at the Monsters Incorporated facility, where he prides himself as being the Lead Scarer. This fine establishment is the sole provider of energy for Monstropolis. The fuel for this society? The screams of innocent children.

One normal work day, Waternoose, the CEO of Monsters Incorporated, offers Sully an opportunity to show a few recruits how to frighten children the right way.

Nothing could interrupt Sully's steady stream of success.

Because Sully is such a good employee, he even does Mike Wazowski a favor and lets him off of work early. While Sully finds some of Mike's paperwork, he encounters a random door that appears like it was leftover from the day's scarings. It's a white door with pink flowers. Definitely a little girl's room. In order to figure out why the door was left in place after hours, Sully investigates and enters the door. He leaves it open—which is one of the worst things to do because a human could invade Monstropolis. Realizing that no one was in the child's room, he leaves the room and shuts the door, and returns to the scare floor. Then, Thud... Thud...Thud...It was Sully's worst nightmare. A little girl playing with his tail!

Sully is one of the bigger, more terrifying guys... but for some reason, this little pig-tailed cutie doesn't see the fear he could instill in her; all she sees is a big tenderhearted animal that she names Kitty as Sully gifts her with the name Boo. Boo is innocent, pure, and authentic. She doesn't understand who she's hanging out with; all she knows is that she is safe with Sully and that she loves him.

Boo has no idea about the world of monsters and that their society's economy is supported by scaring children. All she knows is that Sully looks like a big, trusted, fluffy animal and that she feels nice and safe around him.

Then, it was time to exemplify his prowess to the new recruits. He doesn't know what to do with Boo because to monsters, humans were viewed as the black plague, so he disguises her as a little monster.

Innocent and sweet, Boo witnesses the rip-roaring terror of Sully's scare during the recruit simulator session. All that she thought he was had been thwarted by his terrifying act. No longer was he a big fluffy animal, but a scary monster that most children fear live under their beds. Her whole world was shaken. She trusted Sully and did not look back, but this Kitty was a monster.

One second, she was innocent and fearless, the next? A fearful child without comfort, safety, or protection within the confines of this monster-run world. It was like something special was taken from her.

Sully looks at the video recording of his prestigious performance and sees the utter damage he does to Boo.

Have you ever given your trust, your whole heart to someone, and then all of a sudden you are thrown off guard? Like the rug was ripped right from beneath you? If you have ever felt like Boo, this one is for you. If you have ever been like Sully, causing damage to someone so precious, I challenge you to look at the damage you've done, deal with it and own your part—but know that if you do this, God can redeem you, too.

If you're like Boo, fleeing from your Sully and keeping yourself from her or him is probably first on your mind. That is completely understandable. Protecting yourself from more pain like that is valid. Maybe this person is someone you thought would hold your heart and guard it well. It's usually those people, isn't it? The people that we love the most tend to hurt us the most.

Maybe something has happened in your life that was unexpected, and it set you off course. I don't have all the answers, but what I do know, without a shadow of a doubt, is that you are loved. God will never leave you in your pain.

If you find yourself like Boo, run to the safe arms of Jesus. And I will be praying that you will be restored. It may take time, or it may not, but be assured that if you run to Jesus, He will draw near to you, because "If your heart is broken, you'll find God right there; if you feel like you've been kicked in the gut, He'll help you catch your breath" (Psalm 34:18, MSG).

Let God be your big fluffy Kitty, let Him hold you and protect you, let Him fight for you as you rest and allow Him to restore your broken heart.

REAL STEEL (2011)

The Lord will fight for you; you need only to be still. Exodus 14:14 NIV

Beneath it all, Max just wanted to be with his daddy.

The relationship between a father and a child is very precious. For out of a father comes a child's understanding of their worth. A big question that children ask is: Am I worth the love of my father? When a child's dad is absent by any means, something deep is missing inside their heart.

In this film, we follow Charlie Kenton, a gambler and promoter in the robot boxing arena. He is a struggling man, no longer living in his pro boxing glory days. We see him desperately gambling on the largely expensive robots that he purchases to fight with, and losing each and every time. He's living out of his trailer, drinking plenty of beer, living as a nomad, and indebted to a bunch of people due to his wishful thinking. One day, out of happenstance, Charlie finds out that his ex-girlfriend has passed away, leaving him with Max, his forgotten eleven-year-old son.

Because he is the closest living relative, Charlie must show up in court to settle the custody of his kid. He has one thing on his mind: "How do I get out of this situation?" Aunt Debra and her wealthy husband want to adopt Max. But only for a price. Charlie values Max at $100,000 and the wealthy husband comes to an agreement. Once Aunt Debra and her hubby come back from their summer trip to Italy, then Max would be theirs.

Imagine that. Imagine your father selling you off to someone else. Caring more about himself and his failing robot boxing career than he does you. For some, this might sound familiar.

Per Charlie's usual business, Max's passion for robots forces him to come along while his father's mission is to make money through gambling on robots. Although tough and neglected, and maybe even unknown to himself, Max yearns for his father's attention and acceptance. Charlie ignores Max's recommendations and passionate pleas for his dad's attention and listening ears. If you've seen this film, and you've been through similar stuff, you may have identified closely with this eleven-year-old. Fighting for yourself through the rain and mud, only being protected to a small extent by your father or mother, you might relate. If this resonates for you, it can be painful, but please know there is hope.

Regardless of how Charlie views his "annoying little nuisance," Max turns out to be good luck when he discovers Atom, a basic yet durable robot, who takes them to World Robot Boxing, the most elite fighting league. The irresponsible baby daddy—kid duo eventually merges into father-son champions.

"And I know you had a bum ride Max, and I wasn't there and I should have been...and I can't get those years back Max, but I'm here right now, and if you're up for it, I'm ready to fight."

Their robot, Atom, versus the most illustrious robot, Zeus. It was the showdown of a lifetime as underdog went against beast.

All that Max had read about his father's fighting career, he was finally seeing in person. Max was finally seeing what he hadn't seen in his eleven years of life. In their moment of victory over Zeus, Max was able to look past all of Charlie's failures and embrace him in both pride and love, calling him dad.

Anyone can change. There is always time for restoration.

God can bring restoration and healing to your significant relationships. This restoration may not always mean that the person will change, but it can. The first step to this—go to your Heavenly Dad, receive His worth, His love, His affection and acceptance. Grieve with Him, let Him fill that void, let Him guide you in restoration. Then, when you are ready, keep loving that person, work on forgiveness, look past their weakest moments, but do this while knowing that Jesus validates the pain they have caused you, while leaning on the Father's strength. The person you're thinking about is worth it, and restoration, although sometimes slow, is possible. If this relationship has felt like a boxing round against Zeus, know that there is always a chance for a comeback.

STAR WARS EPISODE V: THE EMPIRE STRIKES BACK (1980)

Every good and perfect gift is from above,
coming down from the Father of the
heavenly lights, who does not change like
shifting shadows. James 1:17 NIV

All fathers are broken, regardless of whether they've been there for you or not.

Luke Skywalker was an innocent farm boy who had a lot of light in him. He also had a destiny—to be a Jedi. When you are pursuing something you feel you are meant to do, it's helpful to know that there are people around who support you. Luke has Obi-Wan and Yoda, but his father was distant. Shocking it was when he hears that his father is Darth Vader, a merciless man filled with darkness. All of Luke's hopes for having a great father dissipated.

We've all heard the quote: "Luke, I am your father." But do we remember the painful scream of Luke yelling "NOOO!" once he hears the news? And do we remember that right before Darth Vader tells Luke that he is his father, Vader cuts off Luke's hand?! Talk about daddy issues.

Luke, akin to the light, was probably ashamed that his own father followed the dark side and was a killer of innocent lives. Finding out that his dad was bad was definitely painful for Luke, and he probably couldn't even wrap his head around the idea. Luke is faced with the harsh reality that a man who commits so much evil could be his father.

Darth Vader's absence in Luke's life clearly leaves a scar.

Maybe you've been deeply hurt by your dad.

STAR WARS EPISODE V: THE EMPIRE STRIKES BACK

Whether your father is there for you or not, your Heavenly Dad is always here, and He never changes. He is consistent, His mood doesn't swing, He isn't aggressive, and He is safe. He is gentle, loving, and you don't have to strive for His time, support, or acceptance.

The truth is, you have a Daddy who loves you. He is THE perfect Dad. He literally knows everything about you and loves you seamlessly. So go to your Heavenly Father who is gentle, kind, and compassionate. Let Him be your Dad and allow Him to take care of you. Let God speak over you. Hear Him fill in your name: "_____ I am your Father. I love you, I am never going to leave you, or forsake you."

Your Heavenly Father will restore you, guide you, and comfort you. Be proud of your Heavenly Father, He won't bring you shame.

SINISTER (2012)

For where your treasure is, there your heart
will be also. Matthew 6:21 NIV

Ellison Oswalt is an author looking to write his next big crime novel. He becomes so obsessed with attaining success that it leads him down a spiraling path of losing his sanity and his family.

Have you ever wanted to be so successful that you were willing to do anything to get there? So willing that you neglected the more important things around you? Maybe even so eager to attain that thing that "gives you life" that you lost everything?

"I just need another hit, just one more."

Ellison, being at a low point of his writing career, desperately hopes for some sort of "break" by purchasing the house of a previously murdered family. Yes…he is that obsessed with his writing. He hopes to analyze the house and the murder in order to come up with that next big story. He is so desperate that he doesn't even tell his family that they will be moving in to such a disturbing home.

"If you miss out on these years with the kids, you won't get them back."

As Ellison strenuously investigates the murder, he reverts back to his radical obsession with writing a successful true-crime novel, which causes the foundation of his marriage to crumble, and in turn leads his family to a life of tragedy and fatal demise.

This film shows that we could lose focus on what is near and dear to us when we place a greater emphasis on other, less important motives. What makes this movie so horrifying is the fact that Ellison loses his family in his search for success. As Ellison hopelessly searches for success, he spots a break in the case of the past family that lived in his home—Bagul. Normally, this sight would lead someone to withdraw, but Ellison was hooked. This could lead to his next big break and his "15 minutes of fame." And as he discovered more and more about the murder, the monster (Bagul) got bigger and bigger. All of it was taking over his life, making him obsessed.

What is more important to you, getting ahead or your commitment and love for God and others? Because where your treasure is, there your heart will be as well.

What do you treasure most? What is most important to you? Your family or your work? Relationships or your success? Your ministry or your family? What's going to really last you in this life? Is your work going to last you? Is that the most important thing in your life? Treasure the right things. Treasure God, and don't forget about others around you. Life is not about power, money, or fame... it's about impacting others around you, and that should begin with those you hold most dear. It's about loving God and loving others.

That is what is going to last you. Don't lose focus of that.

The truth is, we're all famous. Ellison's obsession to attain fame in the eyes of many was fleeting. They wouldn't satisfy him. Attainment of success and fame wouldn't quench his thirst. We see it; he thirsted and thirsted until his own thirst destroyed his family and himself.

You are famous in God's eyes. You don't have to work for it in any way (I mean He calls us to work, to put forth effort, to care about excellence, but don't let this become more important than Him or others. Keep Him number one, people second, and then your work). His eyes are always on you, and He sees all of who you are. There are people who have serious amounts of followers, likes, or subscribers on social media these days, and our society deems them famous. The truth is that everyone is famous. No matter how many people follow you or want to see what you're up to next, none of that matters. What matters is that God is your subscriber. He has a keen following on your life. God is interested in your daily life. He is watching you with an eye of admiration. If your life were a YouTube video, God would click the Like button over and over. How much of a following would that be? Think about it: the most loving, genuine, attractive Creator likes you. Let that satisfy you and let the rest fall into place.

DOCTOR STRANGE (2016)

*The very credentials these people are waving
around as something special, I'm tearing up
and throwing out with the trash—along with
everything else I used to take credit for. And
why? Because of Christ...*
Philippians 3:7-9 MSG

May this idea encourage you today: that there is hope
for everyone. That no matter how hard or prideful a
heart may be, Jesus can soften it.

Doctor Stephen Strange prides himself in being the
most prestigious neurosurgeon there is. His skills are
unlike any other.

One rainy night, his whole world changed. Doctor
Strange begins speeding through the streets in a
Lamborghini as he scrolls through prospective surgical

opportunities to further his fame-mongering career. Heading to a fancy speaking engagement, Strange cuts off the car in front of him, causing him to crash and for his car to explode. These events would blast Strange into a whirling abyss forever altering his life.

Unconscious and in need of immediate surgery, Strange suffers severe damage to the precious instruments which caused him to achieve medical miracles— his hands.

"You've ruined me."

Now unable to use his hands and stripped of his acclaimed success, Stephen sells everything he has to find a cure, coming up empty handed and feeling worthless.

In desperate search of an impossible cure, Strange travels to Kamar-Taj, not exactly willing to forsake his scientific world view but desperate enough to get what he wanted. Motivated by the fact that he could be helped, he meets the Ancient One.

His spiritual eyes are now open, and he'd never be the same again. His resistance to all things emotional or spiritual was slowly caving as he began to train with the Ancient One and honing the craft of mystic arts, in hopes to become a sorcerer. Being maimed was something outside of his own control, bigger than his prideful, puffed up, giant self. It is because of his impairment, that he changed, that his whole world was now one filled with magic and endless possibilities.

"It's not about you." -In my opinion the greatest quote from the film.

It embodies the spirit of what Doctor Stephen Strange's key problem was: his pride. He needed to realize that it was not about accolades, money, or status but being a hero for others, serving them, and saving them. Strange's transformation reminds me a lot of the story about Saul of Tarsus.

Saul was the best religious guy out there, "circumcised on the eighth day, of the people of Israel, of the tribe of Benjamin, a Hebrew of Hebrews; in regard to the law, a Pharisee; as for zeal, persecuting the church; as for righteousness based on the law, faultless" (Philippians 3:5-6, NIV). He was the epitome of a religious zealot. Oh, and he also helped kill Christians.

With a flash of light, Saul's world turned upside down. Blinded by Jesus Himself, Saul lost everything in his blindness, so that when his eyes opened, his transformation was so intense, that his name changed from Saul to Paul. Paul became a man who proclaimed God's word and used love as his weapon.

How does someone like Saul become one of the greatest influencers of the early Church? Transformation. Jesus, the true Teacher, shifts Saul's pride and arrogance into humility and compassion. No longer a bigot, zealot, or prideful jerk, Paul is transformed.

That's truly magical.

God can take *anyone* and make them new, give them a complete 180. If He transformed a killer of Christians, so set on the law who prided himself in his own righteousness, He can humble anyone, transform their lives, and change their identity for His sake. Be thankful that no matter who you are, no matter what you have done, God loves you and has no interest in letting you stay put in your old ways. Pray for the Saul in your life (maybe you are a Saul—if so, pray that Jesus would soften your heart, and make you a new creation), that their world would change and their eyes would open to the glory of God.

THE PRESTIGE (2006)

*Give thanks in all circumstances; for this is
God's will for you in Christ Jesus.*
1 Thessalonians 5:18 NIV

Okay, this movie is extremely complex. The reason why? Jealousy, competition, revenge, and obsession with success lead to big huge, horrific messes and intense amounts of confusion.

This movie plays out like a magic trick. Secrets take place, as well as wonderful illusions and stunning performances from the great Robert Angier and Alfred Borden. A failed attempt at a collaborative magic trick kills Angier's wife, thus severing their friendship, which sparks the genesis of intense competition that roots itself in revenge, jealousy, and obsession with superiority for these two cutting-edge magicians.

Angier is distraught yet amazed at a new trick performed by Borden in which he disappears out of thin air and he reappears (SPOILER ALERT: it's really his twin that's reappearing, and because of their combined identity as both being Borden). With Angier's failed attempts at measuring up to Borden's trick by using a 'double,' he sets out on a more diabolical path to avenge his wife's death. Driven by the need to upstand Borden, Angier embarks on a journey to Nikola Tesla. Angier and Tesla are alike in the fact that they are both success junkies. Tesla warns him that these ultimate pursuits for success may destroy him. Despite the warnings, Angier plans to use one of Tesla's electric blue shock cloning machines to perfect his trick and potentially make him the best "magician" of all time.

Angier performs a trick that no one has ever imagined. Blue electricity zaps him into a trap door as he begins to drown. Seconds later, Angier reappears. It's not him though—Tesla's zapper has given him the actual ability to clone himself. Each time he performs the trick, Angier dies. His fatal obsession with avenging his wife's death and proving himself to be the superior magician paves the way to his own tragic ending.

As if jealousy and revenge didn't end there, Borden is accused of killing Angier, is executed in prison, and the other Borden's wife hangs herself, and then that Borden shoots Angier, and then the movie ends ambiguously with Angier's clone floating in water... sounds like a mess right? It's all because it's rooted in comparison, jealousy, and self-preservation.

If you've seen this movie, then you know there is a lot to unpack, but what I would like to focus on here is the concept of jealousy.

If you 'give in' to envy and jealousy, some nasty things can happen and *the only* recovery from a life of comparison is thankfulness.

Be the best you can be. Don't let your motive to thrive become a motive to one-up, or be better, cooler, and more exciting than others. Strive to make others better around you.

The lesson here is, if you give in to envy or in to wanting what another person has, you end up losing yourself, and it can even have horrific effects on those you love. We all know that jealousy can make us do some nasty things (whether only in our hearts/minds, or actually by doing them—both are toxic).

Have you ever said to yourself, "Why isn't my life as easy as their life? I mean here I am, striving for something, when there are people who don't do much and are rewarded." Borden had a twin, which made his magic appear effortless. Desperation and comparison caused Angier to clone himself.

When you're jealous of what someone else has, you start to lose focus on the importance of what you have and where you are. You are where you are for a reason, be thankful for that.

Don't be jealous, be thankful. Be thankful for the person and the rewards they've been given. When someone else succeeds around you and you're left without success, be thankful for them. It's like a birthday party, celebrate them, don't be the child that cries because you're not the one receiving the gifts. If you get jealous of someone and what they are achieving or what they might have, be thankful to God for them. This truly helps treat the issue of jealousy. Simply pray and be thankful for that person. It's pretty simple. Be thankful for them.

In the midst of jealousy, don't be like Borden or Angier and give in to revenge, but remain thankful for where you are at, don't compare.

Before destruction takes place, choose the route of being thankful for those who excel around you, and remember to be thankful for where you are at. Being thankful is the best cure for envy and comparison. Simply be thankful for where you are at, and what you have, then be thankful for that person, where they're at, and what they have, and pray that God would bless them. Practice this any time a feeling of jealousy rises up inside of you.

JESUS LOVES MOVIES

Comparison is costly and it leads to jealousy. Revenge is birthed in jealousy, but thankfulness leads to the prevention of destruction.

THE GIFT (2015)

*Search me, God, and know my heart; test me
and know my anxious thoughts. See if there
is any offensive way in me and lead me in
the way everlasting. Psalm 139:23-24 NIV*

Do your past sins come back to haunt you? If they do,
it's time to confess them. (Hold on…some of you
might be really tempted to skip this page, dealing with
these things is not easy, but please, please, keep reading).
Have you kept them locked in secret, yet the door keeps
opening on its own? This film represents what happens
if you don't deal with your junk: it never leaves you and
it comes back to bring your life terror.

Simon and Robyn seem like the perfect couple.
They've just purchased a new home and are thriving as a
young married pair. Their life looks picture perfect.

As the film progresses, though, we see that it is not picture perfect. The movie unveils soon into its beginning that there are skeletons in Simon's closet, and that Simon has secrets, secrets in the form of a man named Gordo.

Simon "randomly" reencounters Gordo in a homegoods store. Simon had not seen Gordo since high school, actually. Like the arrogant jerk he had once been, it took time for Simon to register how he knew Gordo. Hidden in their exchange was the secret. After some time, Robyn interrogates her husband, and, slowly, she understands who Gordo is and also realizes that Simon is still the deviant bully he had been as a teenager. We learn that while in high school, Simon spread a nasty rumor that Gordo had been molested by a male student and was gay. This lie resulted in Gordo almost being lit on fire by his prejudiced father. It was the worst time of Gordo's life. He was an easy target and desperately hurt by the rumor that Simon spread.

Through his wife's investigation of his past, Simon doesn't see how what he did was wrong and he acts as if everything is under control, meanwhile he has no control.

Gordo makes multiple attempts to let bygones be bygones, but it is very clear that he's scarred. He makes unsolicited visits bearing extravagant gifts to Simon and Robyn's new home. They feel threatened, and with some admonishment from his wife, Simon attempts to apologize to Gordo. He fails, because he is still a bully. Gordo says: "You're done with the past, but the past is not done with you." Upon hearing this, Simon dominates Gordo by pressing his head to the pavement. Gordo lies there as a victim, a victim of the past, and a victim of the present. After all these years, Simon is still a bully, and Gordo, a victim.

I hear countless stories of people who are oblivious to themselves being bullies and the damage they cause to someone else. There's a way out of this. It starts with confessing.

You may feel as if even though you've said the sinner's prayer, you're set, but there are secrets that you are willing to bring to the grave. You may even have secrets you are willing to keep from people who you know confessing to them would bring you release. Is that freedom? Is that demonstrating the true Gospel? Your level of freedom is equal to your level of confession. If you confess it all, you receive all the freedom, humility, and purity. If you hide it, it will come back to your life like Gordo did to Simon's.

There's no secret that is too embarrassing to God. God is not disappointed in you, and He's not angry with you.

We all have a past. Because of our past, we may develop problems with forgiveness or moving forward. The solution to these problems is confession. It is the only answer.

The question is, are you willing to take that step to move forward? Jesus calls you to be free from captivity and wants you to move forward in freedom.

Are you willing to confess your secrets to Jesus, and to people? There is nothing that takes Him by surprise. God will always forgive you, and He is always eager to begin your restoration process. God is gentle, He is not forceful. He is interested in helping you to no longer identify yourself by your past. Will you share your hidden secrets with Him? Will you let Him gracefully, respectfully, and gently bring healing and light to that deep dark place?

CINDERELLA (2015)

I am my beloved's and my beloved is mine...
Song of Solomon 6:3 NIV

In many ways we are like Cinderella, estranged to the world and left as an orphan. Deep down, our sweet, royal friend Cinderella was probably wishing for someone to save her from the grasp of her evil step-family. She was probably even perplexed and heartbroken at how it all happened. She had lived a life that was filled with love and safety. But with her family dead, she was left helpless and shoved to the side.

"Dirty Ella!"

There is a lot in Cinderella's life that bears incredible similarities to our own. She had once been completely safe and was utterly loved and treasured by her royal family. Sounds like the Garden of Eden, where God had a desire for us to live in a perfect world with Him. But this opportunity was taken from us because of our faults. She then went from being associated with the identity and name of Ella, to being framed with the name, *Cinderella*, an alternative to basically being called worthless ash. Like Cinderella, we were once tainted by the fall of man which we see in the Bible in Genesis 2. We have been searching for redemption, for someone that can save us, and so was Cinderella.

You ever think Cinderella wondered how she went from being a daughter in a great home with her loving family to being treated like a slave? Despite the innocent purity that she holds throughout the film, I think deep down within her, she was desiring someone to save her from her prison-like reality.

"I have to see her again."-Prince Charming

Even with the aftermath of Eden, God develops a plan to save us from sin. His love is so fierce for us, that He says, "I have to be with them again!" He has been

pursuing us every step of the way, since the beginni
flawed humankind.

Prince Charming reminds me of God because
offers Cinderella a life of love and freedom from th
slavery of her wicked stepfamily. His actions really
portray a beautiful picture of what Jesus has done for
you, that while you were once blemished by sin, Jesus
comes, cleans you, and makes you new. How's that for
a love pursuit!? A Prince comes, saves you, and dances
with you. Jesus is the lover of your soul. He takes you
and brings you into the glorious freedom of being
Abba's child. Jesus came to live and die on earth not
just to adopt you into His family, but so that He could be
with you again, the way He wanted it, when He initially
made Eden.

Just like Cinderella, you were an outcast for a Prince
to find, and the radical thing is, God is still pursuing
you. He wants to walk in Eden with you, He wants Eden
restored.

are no longer dusting floors, taking
vil stepmother, or flaws of this world.
im save you, you get to be born again
Family, a family of love and safety.

u know how much God loves you? He died
ble death just for you in order to set you free.
Literally, out of love! That's what motivated
to suffer, to let sharp nails break through His skin,
is bones, His ligaments, to be the One who sacrificed
Himself as the ultimate sin offering, so we wouldn't have
to work tirelessly as slaves when we mess up. LOVE.

God has been pursuing you from the very beginning.
Meditate on the fact that you were once an orphan, but
He has taken you and called you His child. We all want
to be wanted and sought after, just like Cinderella. The
good news is, you've got a Prince Charming who wants
to be with you, who pursues you. With God, the slipper
always fits, and you'll always belong in His family.

THE WIZARD OF OZ (1939)

*Meanwhile we groan, longing to be clothed
instead with our heavenly dwelling, because
when we are clothed, we will not be found
naked. 2 Corinthians 5:2-3 NIV*

We live in a world that needs a heavenly invasion.
It's filled with sin, pain, and brokenness. It needs
restoration.

After being swept up in a tornado, Dorothy of
Kansas, ends up in front of the Yellow Brick Road in
the whimsical Land of Oz—a world filled with creatures
both good and evil, nothing like her home.

Oz was nothing like Dorothy thought over the rainbow
would be like. As a result, she becomes desperately
homesick. She misses home so much that she sets out on

a journey to seek out the works of the powerful Wizard of Oz. The Lion, The Scarecrow, and The Tinman are all missing either courage, a brain, or a heart...but there is a big difference to what Dorothy is missing. She is missing something deep. Why is she longing for home? Because Oz is nothing like Kansas.

The world of Oz is a parallel to the world we live in, where there is pain, brokenness, and heartbreak.

I'm convinced that Dorothy was aching for Kansas with every second she witnessed the darkness of Oz. She just wanted to be home, a sweet place where she belongs.

We are different though.

Although at times it is hard, we don't have to struggle with the dilemma of longing for home and waiting to go home!

We can actually experience a sense of home here on earth, and also bring that sense with us everywhere we go.

What if we had a heart like Dorothy's? Yearning for home with every step that we took? Dorothy has nothing but Toto as a reminder of home while in Oz.

There's one thing about being homesick and thinking about going home, but what if you sought after Jesus until you experienced the peace, love, restoration, and redemption of heaven here on earth? That is what Jesus prayed, for God's kingdom to come on earth.

In heaven, there will be no more pain, sorrow, or sin. I want to encourage you to bring heaven with you on this earth everywhere you go, to allow the fragrance of heaven—love, restoration, and redemption—to be attractive to others, so that they too experience heaven on earth.

Dorothy's dilemma was that she wanted to go back home so badly. But you, you have direct access to home. In a world filled with pain, bring healing. In a world filled with death, bring life. In a world filled with a wicked enemy, stand against his attacks. I challenge you to be a home bringer everywhere you go because there truly is no place like home.

May your desire for heaven propel you to first seek after Jesus, the Provider of peace, redemption, healing, and love, and then be a citizen of heaven to those all around you. When you feel like you're living in a dark world like Oz, choose to pursue Jesus in order to be the light that makes this place look more like home.

Writing this book was literally therapy for me. If in any way you connected with it, I would love to hear your thoughts.

Also, if you have any questions or need a listening ear, you can email me at:
jesuslovesmoviesbook@gmail.com

Website: www.JesusLovesMovies.com

Social Media: @philthatin
Facebook, Twitter, Instagram

Ant-Man. Dir. Peyton Reed. Perf. Paul Rudd, Michael Douglas, Evangeline Lilly, and Corey Stoll. Marvel Studios. 2015.

The Babadook. Dir. Jennifer Kent. Perf. Essie Davis, Noah Wiseman, and Hayley McElhinney. Babadook Films, Causeway Films, South Australian Film Corporation, and Screen Australia. 2014.

Cinderella. Dir. Kenneth Branagh Perf. Lily James, Cate Blanchett, and Richard Madden. Walt Disney Pictures. 2015.

The Count of Monte Cristo. Dir. Kevin Reynolds. Perf. Jim Caviezel, Guy Pearce, Dagmara Dominczyk, and Richard Harris. Touchstone Pictures. 2002.

Doctor Strange. Dir. Scott Derrickson. Perf. Benedict Cumberbatch, Chiwetel Ejiofor, Rachel McAdams, Benedict Wong, Mads Mikkelsen, and Tilda Swinton. Marvel Studios. 2016.

Frozen. Dir. Chris Buck and Jennifer Lee. Perf. Kristen Bell, Idina Menzel, Jonathan Groff, Josh Gad, and Santino Fontana. Walt Disney Pictures. 2013.

The Gift. Dir. Joel Edgerton. Perf. Jason Bateman, Rebecca Hall, and Joel Edgerton. STX Entertainment/Blumhouse. 2015.

Groundhog Day. Dir. Harold Ramis. Perf. Bill Murray, Andie MacDowell, and Chris Elliot. Columbia Pictures. 1993.

Guardians of The Galaxy. Dir. James Gunn. Perf. Chris Pratt, Zoe Saldana, Dave Bautista, Vin Diesel, and Bradley Cooper. Marvel Studios. 2014.

Hacksaw Ridge. Dir. Mel Gibson. Perf. Andrew Garfield, Sam Worthington, Luke Bracey, Teresa Palmer, Hugo Weaving, Rachel Griffiths and Vince Vaughn. Summit Entertainment. 2016.

Inside Out. Dir. Pete Docter and Ronnie Del Carmen. Perf. Amy Poehler, Phyllis Smith, Bill Hader, Lewis Black, Kaitlyn Dias, Kyle MacLachlan and Diane Lane. Walt Disney Pictures. 2015.

Mean Girls. Dir. Mark Waters. Perf. Lindsay Lohan, Jonathan Bennett, Rachel McAdams, and Tina Fey. Paramount Pictures. 2004.

Monsters Inc. Dir. Pete Docter, David Silverman, and Lee Unkrich. Perf. John Goodman, Billy Crystal, and Mary Gibbs. Walt Disney Pictures. 2011.

A Place Beyond the Pines. Dir. Derek Cianfrance. Perf. Ryan Gosling, Bradley Cooper, Eva Mendes, Mahershala Ali, and Ben Mendelsohn. Sidney Kimmel Entertainment/Verisimilitude. 2012.

The Prestige. Dir. Christopher Nolan. Perf. Hugh Jackman, Christian Bale, Michael Caine, Rebecca Hall, and Scarlett Johansson. Touchstone Pictures and Warner Bros. 2006.

Ratatouille. Dir. Brad Bird and Jan Pinkava. Perf. Patton Oswalt, Ian Holm, Lou Romano, and Janeane Garofalo. Walt Disney Pictures. 2007.

Real Steel. Dir. Shawn Levy. Perf. Hugh Jackman, Dakota Goyo, and Evangeline Lilly. Dreamworks Pictures. 2011.

The Revenant. Dir. Alejandro G. Iñárritu. Perf. Leonardo DiCaprio, Tom Hardy, Domhnall Gleeson, and Forrest Goodluck. 20th Century Fox, Regency Enterprises, and Ratpac Entertainment. 2015.

The Rookie. Dir. John Lee Hancock. Perf. Dennis Quaid and Rachel Griffiths. Walt Disney Pictures. 2002.

The Sandlot. Dir. David Mickey Evans. Perf. Tom Guiry, Mike Vitar, Patrick Renna, Denis Leary and James Earl Jones. Twentieth Century Fox. 1993.

Shawshank Redemption. Dir. Frank Darabont. Perf. Tim Robbins, Morgan Freeman, Bob Gunton, William Sadler, and Clancy Brown. Castle Rock Entertainment. 1994.

Sinister. Dir. Scott Derrickson. Perf. Ethan Hawke, Juliet Rylance, Michael Hall D'Addario, Claire Foley, and James Ransone. Summit Entertainment, Alliance Films, and Blumhouse Productions. 2012.

Spider-Man: Homecoming. Dir. Jon Watts. Perf. Tom Holland, Michael Keaton, Robert Downey Jr., Marisa Tomei, and Zendaya. Columbia Pictures/Marvel Studios. 2017.

Split. Dir. M. Night Shyamalan. Perf. James McAvoy, Anya Taylor-Joy, Betty Buckley, Haley Lu Richardson, and Jessica Sula. Universal Pictures. 2017.

Star Wars Episode V: The Empire Strikes Back. Dir. Irvin Kershner. Perf. Mark Hamill, Harrison Ford, Carrie Fisher, Billie Dee Williams, and Frank Oz. Lucasfilm. 1980.

Toy Story. Dir. John Lasseter. Perf. Tom Hanks, Tim Allen, Don Rickles, Wallace Shawn, and John Ratzenberger. Walt Disney Pictures/Pixar Animation Studios. 1995.

The Wizard of Oz. Dir. Victor Fleming. Perf. Judy Garland, Frank Morgan, Ray Bolger, Bert Lahr, Jack Haley, Billie Burke, and Margaret Hamilton. Metro-Goldwyn-Mayer (MGM). 1939.

Wonder Woman. Dir. Patty Jenkins. Perf. Gal Gadot, Chris Pine, Robin Wright, Connie Nielsen, Danny Huston, and David Thewlis. Warner Bros. 2017.

Wreck-It Ralph. Dir. Rich Moore. Perf. John C. Reilly, Jack McBrayer, Sarah Silverman, Jane Lynch, and Alan Tudyk. Walt Disney Pictures. 2012.

Zootopia. Dir. Byron Howard, Rich Moore, and Jared Bush. Walt Disney Pictures. 2016.

CPSIA information can be obtained
at www.ICGtesting.com
Printed in the USA
BVHW031447301221
625228BV00006B/483

9 780692 155059